Your Universe

Walter C. Lanyon

Kessinger Publishing's Rare Reprints

Thousands of Scarce and Hard-to-Find Books on These and other Subjects!

- Americana
- Ancient Mysteries
- Animals
- Anthropology
- Architecture
- Arts
- Astrology
- Bibliographies
- Biographies & Memoirs
- Body, Mind & Spirit
- Business & Investing
- Children & Young Adult
- Collectibles
- Comparative Religions
- Crafts & Hobbies
- Earth Sciences
- Education
- Ephemera
- Fiction
- Folklore
- Geography
- Health & Diet
- History
- Hobbies & Leisure
- Humor
- Illustrated Books
- Language & Culture
- Law
- Life Sciences
- Literature
- Medicine & Pharmacy
- Metaphysical
- Music
- Mystery & Crime
- Mythology
- Natural History
- Outdoor & Nature
- Philosophy
- Poetry
- Political Science
- Science
- Psychiatry & Psychology
- Reference
- Religion & Spiritualism
- Rhetoric
- Sacred Books
- Science Fiction
- Science & Technology
- Self-Help
- Social Sciences
- Symbolism
- Theatre & Drama
- Theology
- Travel & Explorations
- War & Military
- Women
- Yoga
- *Plus Much More!*

We kindly invite you to view our catalog list at:
http://www.kessinger.net

"THIS is my Universe," said the ancient Greek, and then inscribed over the portal of his temple " Know thyself." He who knows himself rightly, knows God. Can there be more than God in a universe of God ? Can there be God and anything else if God fills all space eternally and is changeless ? He who knows himself, knows God, for God is the only Self of the universe. As man comes to understand this, it becomes clear to him that this is indeed his universe.

The old puzzle of where to hide the divinity of man was finally solved by placing it within himself. Man has looked for it everywhere but within himself ; hence it has proved a safe hiding-place. However, he is awakening to the Truth of Being, and is coming to understand that his attitude towards life determines what life will be to him.

A sculptor and a stone-mason see something entirely different in the same piece of stone ; again, two sculptors or two stone-masons looking at the same stone may see entirely different possibilities in it. Everything in the universe, in one sense of the word, is plastic to the consciousness which fashions it, according to the attitude taken towards it ; and yet everything is changeless and eternal in a universe ruled by a changeless Power.

" What is one man's meat is another man's poison " indicates that it is purely a matter of attitude. The same thing that sustains one may kill another, according to the attitude taken towards it. The thing does not change that kills or sustains ; it is merely the attitude that is different. Morphine does not quiet everyone, but has the reverse effect on some people. What cures one man does not cure another, or all disease would have long ago been wiped out by the use of medicine.

The man whom you call a benefactor another may call a devil ; the man remains the same—the difference is in the attitude towards him which causes him to seem to react in accordance with your belief.

A lover sees beauty where you may see homeliness. The story of " Beauty and the Beast " fully illustrates what a change of attitude does towards life. It is a story of your own life. You are always tied up to a beast (problem) before you know that it only awaits the recognition of its better self to change into a Prince Charming. When you can hold to the eternal facts of Being, in spite of appearances, you will see the transformation take place before your very eyes —in the place where you saw lack you will see plenty ; in the place of inharmony, harmony ; in the place of sickness, health. Whatever you love you glorify. You have for ages been seeking the universal panacea.

" Awake thou that sleepeth." " Love never faileth." Love is God, and a quality of God at the same time. It is love which transforms everything. Love is knowledge of life. Belief changes constantly, sentiment changes, and emotions come and go ; but " love never faileth," and never changeth.

Love is the understanding of the *isness* of things. It is a conscious capacity to " see God in temples not made with hands, and eternal in the heavens." You and your neighbours are these temples " not made with hands." " The Lord in the midst of thee is strong and mighty " is a statement of a fact. When you come to understand this as a fact you will see God in every man. Yes, you will see him in everything, even in the thing called space, since he is everywhere, eternally present. Then it naturally follows that the higher your concept of him, the higher and finer your universe and ideas will be.

Your body and universe are only the out-picturing of what you conceive yourself to be. It is the shadow of your soul ; a screen upon which are thrown all the attitudes you hold toward yourself and your universe.

The moment you become conscious of a thing as real and eternal, that thing comes into visibility in the realm of the manifest. The moment you release a thing in consciousness, it is released from the visible world.

" Loose him and let him go " is a command to every man who is holding a worry

HL

attitude toward his temple and his universe. Again the " letting " comes into play. You will finally know that only what you " let " can actually happen.

You can see the invisible become visible before your very eyes by the " letting " process. You have only to " let " a smile loose in your universe to see it caught up and reflected by everyone who comes in contact with it. Everybody understands the language of a smile ; it is universal. Drummond says, " We do not know what ripples of healing are set in motion when we smile on one another."

A smile is a recognition of something higher and finer than most of us imagine. A second before you smile every face may be frowning and serious, but in the twinkling of an eye you see your thought crystallized into realization—the inward state of consciousness becomes the manifest. " That which is told in secret shall be called from the housetop." This proves to you that this is your universe and that it is affected—yes, controlled—by your attitude towards it. Note the difference between a smile and a grin. It is the difference between the real and the unreal ; a grin rarely gets much response, for it is forced and hard to sustain. A grinning face may be hideous and ugly, but a smiling face always has charm.

When you come to understand the " letting," in contradistinction to the " making," you begin to appreciate God's manner of working. There is always a joy in "letting." If those working in the Truth would realize this, they would delete from their consciousness the very serious attitude towards life and cease struggling. No matter how you try, you are not going to force God either to do your bidding or your begging. He cannot do more than he has already done, which is *all*.

You can, however, recognize this fact, and "let" it into expression. Why will the self-styled healer insist that God does the work, and at the same time become so concerned about the outcome of it?

The moment he recognizes the fact that life is spiritual he has brought forth the fruits of Spirit, and has dropped off the idea of personal responsibility. He who calls himself a healer and then uses what is known as the "tongs and hammer method" (the beating and fighting to make God answer his prayer), will find that he has plenty of work to do with his "tongs and hammer," and that for every bit of effort he has put forth he has only succeeded in making the condition worse. Putting forth great effort is not knowing the Truth, but foreshadows a great doubt that God is able to fulfil his promises. "If we will be still and know," finally we shall hear some of the statements of Truth and abide in peace.

Who that has heard the Truth can again

designate anyone as " my patient." What is this silly ownership of another? Who are you that you should stamp the branding-iron of possession on another? All this leads to the amusing situation of the circumstance man using methods and means to hold his patients. Imagine what a rich harvest this kind of thought is going to bring when it is time for that person to reap.

In the same way, mysticism is introduced into the teachings by " the holier than thou " attitude of many healers. Trying to make others do your bidding is only saying to yourself that you will make God do your bidding. Woe unto that one who tries to offend the law in this manner. The wrath of God, of his own making, shall grind him to powder. He who through ignorance or wilfulness tries to " steady the ark of another " will find his power " withered away." Look well to this meddlesome state of mind, and let thy brother alone. Speak the word of Truth, but do not try domination. The thing you dominate in one instance will one day dominate you with accelerated force though you may flourish as a " green bay " for a while—all of which brings you to understand that the " wrath of God " is the wrath of your own making. When you instil the doctrine of fear in another you are only instilling it into your own self, and it shall return to you " pressed down and running over."

You are not responsible for the healing of another. You are asked to make a statement of fact to him, to call to his remembrance the Eternal Facts of Being, not to work some magic trick over him.

" I will " is the answer of Spirit to every prayer that is made in true understanding, and it follows " according to your faith be it unto you," and " the servant is healed in the selfsame hour " if he has had the faith to accept the " it-is-done " state of mind.

You are joyously abandoned into life. This is God's universe and he can, and does run it perfectly. You are a point in consciousness. Why not let this power into expression, instead of trying to distort it to personal ends ? Verily it shall be well with thee if God rules in your universe, consciously. " Be still and know." Contemplate the glory of it all ; rest in peace ; it is well with thee.

Prayer is not a means of changing the universe, but a way of getting into line with the Power, " which to know aright is Life Eternal." You have the infinite capacity to become one with this power, and then you shall know what it is to be in a majority. Becoming one with the Power is to feel the divine urge of life, expressing itself through everything and every circumstance. Why should you worry ? Nothing matters.

Give up the foolish idea of trying to change God or his universe to suit your personal demands, and you will find that the universe, for you, is suddenly changed from hell to heaven. "Not my will (personal sense) but thine be done" is not submission to blind fate, but conscious activity into life, because you are guided eternally by the voice of Truth, which says "this is the way, walk thou in it."

Give up striving for freedom and you shall know the joyous abandon of life. Does a lily struggle into expression? Have you considered the lily? If God cannot do it, it cannot be done, so why not rest the case with him, since he has invited you to lean on him and to take the burden of his glorious understanding upon yourself—the understanding that, being spiritual, you are free from the hamperings of material beliefs. God has already done everything that needs to be done. "Be still, be still, be still."

Before you ask the answer *is*, and while you are yet lisping the words it is given unto you. This is what comes of "letting" God express through you, in his glorious way, instead of trying to force him to do your bidding. Oh, the wonder of it, the rest and peace of it all, when you take up your place in the body of Christ, "for we are all members of the one body"; and one member is as important as another. Through all parts of this grand body flows a stream of God ideas, sustaining everything in perfect peace and joy.

And so you are joyously abandoned into

life, for now you know. You are free. Nothing matters. You have recognized the real, and " the lines have fallen to you in pleasant places." Only beliefs and conditions will change, because they are but the objectified thought pictures that change and disintegrate before your very eyes.

Take away your judgment from appearances because in them you are always deceived. When you look at the outside of an egg nothing seems to be happening for weeks, but a new life is forming on the inside. Something is happening from the moment the warmth of the mother love touches the egg ; this is not visible to the appearance world, but the mother love feels it is so. So it is with your problem—every time you meditate upon the *isness* of your Perfect Self something tremendously interesting is taking place on the inside, though the appearance may not indicate it on the outside. One day the shell cracks, and out comes the new idea, perfect and glorious. " For unto us a child is born and his name shall be called Wonderful, the Mighty, the Everlasting," and this child is born in the stable of your heart. Instantly this news is broadcast the Herod idea of the circumstance mind wishes to kill the newborn child.

" Keep silent before me—see that you tell no man."

What matter though the world, judging from appearance, says nothing is happening.

You know that it is, and so you rest in peace; then one day " it is called from the house-tops " and you follow the command, "Launch out into the deep waters " of a new activity. The larger fish are in the deep waters, but until you are of " the seeing eye " and " hearing ear " you are not able " to launch out."

Away with all the foolish wondering whether this or that person will like or dislike what you are doing! Away with all the self-appointed keepers of the Truth who screech out that you are off the track or are following a blind path! *You are never in danger of going far afield if you follow Christ.* Remember that he is for all men, in all climes and under all conditions. The Truth is the thing which is good for everybody at all times.

" Hold fast to that which is good." " Go not back again to your former bondage " once you have tasted the freedom of a dweller in the Finished Kingdom. This *isness* is the kingdom that Jesus came offering to the world, and so few heard the word with the hearing ear; yet what countless thousands are following after the dead letter. " My way is the only way," they say, and they condemn you if you do not follow their way. What of Christ's way? " He that has ears to hear, let him hear." Throw opinions to the wind, and do not listen to the arguments of personal sense or appearance.

Contemplate this Finished Mystery. " Be still and know." Rest in the " peace that passeth all understanding." Rest in Peace. It is well with thee.

Oh, glorious message ! We start now with " It is done," because we recognize that everything must already be done in a Finished Kingdom, and certainly God said, " It is finished " and " good " and he rested. Why not rest awhile in this peace.

" Tarry awhile in Jerusalem (peace)."

This is the end of this publication.

Any remaining blank pages are for our book binding
requirements and are blank on purpose.

To search thousands of interesting publications like this one,
please remember to visit our website at:

http://www.kessinger.net

CPSIA information can be obtained at www.ICGtesting.com
Printed in the USA
LVOW03s0050030115

421320LV00018B/1468/P